EX LIBRIS

"WHO GIVES?
WHO RECEIVES?
IN THE GIFT MOMENT
ONLY TWO HANDS IN
EXCHANGE."

JUDITH LEE STRONACH
25 MAY 1943
29 NOVEMBER 2002
STONEWALL

Judith —

ACROSS THE GREAT DIVIDE

Selected Poems

Thanks for your support!

by
Tobey Kaplan

San Francisco
1995

Copyright © 1995 Androgyne Books

Androgyne Books
930 Shields Street
San Francisco, CA 94132

Photograph on back cover by David Weisman.

Illustrations and the cover by Ellen Woods.

ISBN 1-879594-19-6

Table Of Contents

Acknowledgements

These poems have appeared in slightly different versions in the following publications:

"Somedays" in *Americas Review,* Fall 1992. (she was) Able to Say in *California Poets in the Schools,* 1989. "Waiting Again" in No Turning Back a limited edition chapbook published by e.g. books, San Francisco, 1984. "In the Field/Hafsika" in *Poems on Contemporary Israel* edited by Leah Schweitzer and Elaine Starkman published by the Judah L. Magnes Museum, Berkeley 1990. "Descartes" *Chester H. Jones Foundation Anthology,* 1993.

ACROSS THE GREAT DIVIDE, words and music by Kate Wolf. Permission granted by Another Sundown Publishing Company (BMI) © 1980.

I've been sifting through the layers
of dusty books and faded papers.
They tell a story I used to know;
one that happened so long ago.

Gone away--in yesterday
and I find myself on the mountainside,
Where the rivers change direction
Across the Great Divide.

Kate Wolf

I would like to deeply thank my poetry group, **Word of Mouth** *for their continuing love and support: Grace Grafton, Rusane Morrison, Rob Stewart, Carol Dorf, Catherine Freeling, Melissa Kwasny and at various times many others who have dropped in to help with the craft of revision.*

Part One

One star in a murky green pond
then a sea of stars come up over silent orange crests;
today I lost the trail, then found my way
          after a moment of panic.

Mosquitos head for certain death
          as I slap them on my arm
and in the crackle of branches, I call hello to footsteps
and then shine my flashlight and stumble
          out of the tent
to find a mule deer, with large erect ears,
          eating my leftovers
and as I watch it nibble for a while, I imagine this
wilderness roamed by millions of deer,
this one munches thoughtfully then drinks
from the pond.

I look up at the silent stars,
the rumble in my stomach echoes in the tent
a woman somewhere lost on the trail,
a deer felled by a hunter
the tree branch crackling
and the shimmer of light.

SYRACUSE WINTER 1972

I am walking through campus in a snowstorm
on my way to Nadine's, great old buildings
shrouded in swirling flakes and darkness.
I pause on the hill before I descend
the stairs to Crouse Avenue.
Streetlights glitter over the yellow glare of snow.

A single lantern flame in the window
of the upper attic room, she must be painting
she might not be alone.

The air freezes my shadow that strays across snow.
The dormitory down the hill bursts with student music
as cars drift slowly through unplowed roads below.
The edge of night settles in my heart, the lonely world
revolving, creamy mush under my feet. I look up
at the single flame again.

I think of going down the stairs to the street and up
the rickety porch to the doorway
of the shabby gray house to see Nadine.
My hands finger dust crumbling in my pockets.
I turn around into the deep winter silence.

SOMEDAYS

I think about my old friends from college, Carol M.
and Anne Higgins;
as I run the dogs in the morning fog; think make-up,
tooth-decay, with ideas.
At a workshop someone suggested
      "try writing in sentences".

I'd think about it,
as I spend my time with those people
      who already risked,
part of their feelings and what matters
      within stories of violence,
and endangered, their lives will not be long—
I know, some of them ten years younger than me look
ten years older.
Long ago, not so far away perhaps once upon a time,
we lost them.
I see the cars of supplies go into the living units,
stacks of boxes, matches, toilet paper and sanitary
napkins and all the writing paper
for their poems, letters, their somedays and sentences.

One moonlit evening, in downtown Oakland, a woman
asks me for money and adds
how black people are oppressed and she's high on
something it seems,
a flood of light halos and her words suspended
      in cold air,
and how could I ever feel like that she'd be better off
in jail...

where I know the bite of incarceration,
the scars and anger of washed out dignity.

Then I drift back to an upstate snowstorm
a pool table in a sawdust cellar bar
a hillside of words and soft clouds,
a raft in the water of sky.
think about work and "sentence"
Windows shake the throat of night, time,
       lengths of time.

Here's the blank paper "Write your story",
I offer the nourishment of some power,
the parent they wished they had;
sentences are a crusade, not the distorting
       of Satan or Jesus
but the expedition in the name of saving yourself
       with language.

I tell them I went to college, when they ask.
Why do I do this? Maybe the liberal middle class
made me believe I had something to offer,
no training, just the city school,
but poetry and poets taught me the streetcorner,
observe the way a shoe is tied,
the way to avoid or look into someone's eyes.
Somedays I don't want to get involved.

Somedays I wake up with my socks pulled down
and my feet look webbed.
The dishes have to be washed.
The alarm clock buzzing in a dream.
A cold bed full of moonlight.

I fall into this clean sheet bed
after a night on the streets
air shapes my body, hills brush the sky
water disappears in my closed eyes:
I wish I knew someone like myself,
not someone to please, but to help me
with just one life.

you clean out things you've collected
postcards and notes and you have to keep
clinging to the walls
what to give away what you'll never leave

that one curious kiss, urgent and breathful
bashful as if we saw each other naked
and closed our eyes.
birds twitter over the hill and by the freeway
I'm just full of myself
these poems and all the love
I've ever known or invented.

WHAT I LOVE TO REMEMBER

all the faces, familiar, people looking at the ceiling
a clump of heads on the floor, some leftover food
crumpled wax paper, a sip taken from a glass,
the clatter of voices, bells from the cashier,
the squeak of doors, jukeboxes and something I never
hear something I never know.

the churning food in the belly, the awkward smile
creeping across someone's face, entering the friendly
dark together, the smell of food and beer clinging to
their clothes and hair, the clothes falling beside the
bed, smoky eyes rubbing the other's cheek, hair and
skin rising and falling into the familiar breath and
their smiles together

my smile their lips a question, their street, my legs
never near, my heart never close my own silence my
breath slipping through the dark the quiet lights of a
sleeping city as the guy wipes the table and tells me
what time he closes

later there's a woman in bed who knows my heartbeat
and thick socks, her dreamy warmth sliding through
my arms, through the night air my city street
my silent stars and gentle silence

climbing into bed after she falls asleep
into her dream her body an earthy memory
a swampy warmth, a silky smoky pond
where my flanks shiver into the cling of love

there's not a solitude of the mind I would drown
in thoughts if I could only listen to the breath
of the hand that turns the night and loves me

and another hand, desires neighbors of quiet
or far off, a baby pushes open the room
the baby cannot sleep, crawls into the warmth
that embraced this life again
anyone
some stars and dogs barking and the cars fizzle
while bars close down
streets open into forests
sprawled across one day and night
and then I seize covers around me
curl into blossoms of light I know
long ago the world mentioned a word

SMILING A DISTANT HARMONICA

I look for your face to leap out of this poem
after I climb the ridge during a light rain
expecting to see someone I really didn't get to know.

So I gallop into a Western tavern
where you waitress
delivering drinks cracking jokes
with the boys, and at first you think,
I'm just another customer you don't want
and then your face gleams in surprise,
my horse is tied outside and soon, I say,
I have to be going, just stopped in for a beer
where the band and crowd are hooting and clapping
smoky lights dim around us.

The sun slinks low on the prairie
blushing the sky like your cheeks
and I wink at you our secret kiss
that last time we met by chance

on a cruise to a tropical island
when you sat on the steaming deck
in a chaise lounge wearing a very small swimsuit;
you bronze legs glistening from sunlight on water,
and one moment you glanced over to me,
and then to the child hugging the rail and her mother
and you asked what would happen if that child fell in
the whole world drowning along with her
in the panic that seizes her floundering in the sea.

The horror that could redeem our separate
floating all of us, your vision passed through me
a passion you understand as poetry
that we must take what is given to the farthest
extremes to know what is valuable,
the child's hair, sun-bleached,
a shadow of imagination stretched upon the water.

The ship docked in an exotic port
where natives bargained with tourists
and it was possible to escape with lies.
A fancy car waited for you,
and I touched the small of your back
as you passed, then turned for a kiss and I nodded yes
captured by your eyes, as the child
        left with her mother
their friends waving,
and the fog slipped between us all.

I worked for a season
sweating my way back to mainland
traded my sealegs for a horse, who is waiting
while I rest my arms on this glossy table
watch your eyes flicker in the swirl of light
while you tumble through orders of drunks,
men swearing at men, women giggling together.

I ask you to set down your tray and dance
words drowned by music and light,
the edge of foam settling in my glass.
What have you been through to be working here?
I yell, the cruise, the fancy car
and then there's the crashing of glass

and you grab my hand and the horse's reigns
and we ride and ride into the purpling sky
clinging to the horse and each other
we find the city at sunrise glowing,
slowly waking to its day.

Down by the docks, the ship leaves in minutes
and we board with the horse, nodding itself along
as the islands drift through fog and sun
we dissolve in the blue ridge of horizon
smiling a distant harmonica.

the language of love is soliloquy
Olga Broumas

the language of love requires a duet to speak
Colette

you want so much to have a body
to do whatever you tell it
to touch what is wrong
or to leave it alone
Gerard Malanga

You don't ask for much but a lot of it
what's eventually going to knock you off your feet
the earth
the children have the sky
the eyes and smiles of faces we rub together
they watch what we touch
don't think about preparing meals
they climb on us like trees
they wake us and ask why

love has invaded all the rooms
cutting through light
silence, conversation
the mirror's empty shadow of dust
bits of sun kissed in our eyes

at breakfast   kitchen corners
a river, persistence of movements
invention of gravity
words set upon the table
among the dishes

each difficulty that makes us strong,
tender, ragged memory
we press upon each other
gently tearing into
the family history
curious about what we've dreamed

in other words
what we've collected
bits of rock
dried flowers cracking in stale morning
the sky
how everything falls together

NEW BUTTERFLIES MADE OF DUST...

Words take their first steps on the darkness
Of a white page
And when the time comes to rise
Ashes won't let go of our hands
            Jan Kaplinski, translated from Estonian

My frenzied alarm clock and butterflies briefing
            for this morning out the door
and into hazy light, wordless
the neighborhood of unknown houses
desperate relationships knotted trees, sap dripping,
wind and sunlight and this early,
a man stops me for a match
then asks for change as air flows through my fingers.

Yellow peppers on a blue plate in the front yard
shine on a wooden bench as my dog chases a cat down
the driveway; a white man and a black woman
on their tandem bicycle;
a waitress in a red apron and white blouse
gets out of her car,

and there's a midget couple up the street, on their way
to work. A couple of roaddiggers,
insect buzz and plums smashing the sidewalk
my shoes sticking to the pavement; for breakfast
brambleberries coffee brewing, and I'll attempt to
open those folders of poetry, what is mine, what is
theirs, dust beneath my chair.

WHEN CHILDREN ARE IN THE HOSPITAL

There's an ache in the air
a tense smile between grown-ups
balloons and flowers cast long shadows
in curtain-ribbed sunlight
where nurses warm the stethoscope bell
in the palms of their hands before
taking it briskly under bedclothes;
afternoons blur through the trees,
the cars outside rumble quietly muffled
as streets press into themselves
and parents can't remember
      where they parked their car.
Some friend brought over schoolbooks with silent
questions
whispers of lies
no answers.

Part Two

THE BOY TALKING TO A SKULL
from a photograph in National Geographic

The boy is talking to history
speaking the language of the earth
he wants to know what his fathers knew,
the colors of wind, the laughter
        from mountain and cloud
the stories chattered by animals and trees,
the gentle dances sleeping in human hearts.

He asks the skull questions
        he has asked all the others.
He watches the skull tenderly
as if his delight will allow it to speak.
And the skull has the answer:
        the dead have taken the wisdom with them.

Before ragtime, before rage and sadness before gospel
before blues, before the blood rose in their chests-
the gravest injustice is to silence history
        from the children,
when another day another boy will unearth
his quiet skull.

As he listens for the voices of his ancestors,
the boy talks to the wind.

LESSONS OF DARKNESS
from Christian Boltanski

faces fade into memory of possession
tin biscuit boxes
faces under glass light of memory

numbers and faces on boxes
shelves of possessions and walls of clothes
broken lights and angels shadows
revolving

my broken wings
my hands dripping from my elbows
teeth slack in my jaw

children smile into the broken future

tin biscuit boxes
the weapon of memory
that survives whatever it takes
faces fading into photographs
a face that was a child

that light exists for shadow

NEW YORK CITY LATE JANUARY

*"Description which is all we have to give each other
will not attend desperation..."*
                        Patricia Hampl

A shell, humble ambition , desire for memory.
I drink seltzer out of a cup with a horseshoe etched
on the bottom, a glass of wax candle
to light at Yiskor, in memory of the day
a loved one departed. We always light candles
so the spirits will see us and we light their passage
a short term of exile our silent plans.
Three decades have slunk by and my handwriting
worsens
what no one may understand like our times
bombarded with information and unspoken language.
Along the way we divide truth from power
so that the world is pushed along and we get things
done.

The ambivalent city of gray faces and fine arts
the best of tradition and experiment,
where people like to argue
even if no one wins.
Subways full of muggers, victims, vigilantes
where I could intercept a stray bullet,
get in the way of a scuffle of feet.
Words untouchable in the City that conceals
tenderness with lust
Sweet loneliness that begins at night,
each measure the snow crackling underfoot,

the slick ice vibrating in the sun
as a single icicle drips frozen from a branch,
fingers embrace air.

All history as lyric, the music mad voices
that kick the door open for clues so the neighborhoods
are satisfied each morning
where people slowly rise gray exhaust hovers
over curbs trimmed with snow
feet get lost in their steps
we survive light and keep describing
transparent despair and a sense of duty
to what can be said, I am committed to
precision of habit, necessary promises
landscape of brick houses new snow falling
white skies muffled traffic cars swish and slide
people speak louder in New York,
more sure of their opinions
Art that's never easy unless it's mediocre
only if it's talent that you can wish for like fame
gossip is jagged memory
giving the snow something to fall into,
a dry softness and we are surprised when it melts.

The squirrel dashes across the road,
brittle branches with snow dangling
into floating bits of sky
conditions you can never be sure of unless
something catches
a thread pulls loose, seams, uneven
wrinkles when the skin of fabric could be smooth
like creases of a smile, the mouth pursed into regret
or anger the repeat of seasons,

difficult weather we endure, how it changes.
Ambition is never without effort
break of water upon land, where a mist covers thickly
over the inlet
that sky blends into shoreline.

Oils spread over the surface of skin, muscles tighten or
bulge under sweaters. The breath I have mingles into
thoughts, speech, leaves.
Too long to grasp, touch or fondle
In the face of disappointment a whole lot more
the body betrays emotion and stars,
            snowy carved streets
where beaches burn in summer
a blackness echoes through sky and light
torn disaster a bony back slapped against rock
where wind batters the coast and I slip through again,
the space between stars and summer religion,
winter mythology a safety in numbers.

Someone offers me a drink,
people chattering in the next room
eyes that gesture, willing,
I get impatient about the streets
and saturated with conversation, don't try to explain
wet complications, as we linger towards
what shadows blossom.
Delicate frost dusts grass unnoticed like whispers,
around corners and fog, dripping wet gray skies,
I bundle up in clothes and desire something else.

Ice flakes on my wrist
as I reach into the freezer for frozen soup
to defrost in the microwave for dinner.
We rattle wooden chairs
and dishes and move so that we cannot hear
our dog barking down the street.

Then we hear that tense silence,
the echo of the dog, her voice
off in the night distance
and we know that someone is passing by
who shivers, uncertain
and that scares her.

We do not speak while warming leftovers
the air remains cold
although the soup is steaming on the table;

Our dog is at the door
waiting to be let inside.

WITHOUT QUESTION

1.

What I have done or not done
in a moment of longing
someone left me or I decided
I'd forget in a lonely haze
of troubled sleep

any person just passing through
a dog is gone a poem is finished
I'd say tremble

in the dirty air
laundry spills all over the floor of a dream
in Chinese restaurant

there's a family reunion
people who have once been close
miss those things I forgot to do

turn down the heat
it won't work out anyway I'd expect
like an knowing about an airplane
or figuring the time
and what I have to do to get there

I notice the growth of a tree
precisely because of my absence'
the laundry just scattered that way
unreliable drafts of air I replace with words

hazy heat floating over the almost night
until a washrag is hurled through a doorway
and it misses the laundry and lands
            on a pile of newspapers

and all the shoes question my ability to run
down that old street
where the tree had just been planted;
in the beginning of April
I think about my baseball cards
that have been missing for over twenty years.

knowing that one person isn't a pivot
but a question

2.

One morning on a hill, I noticed a man
sleeping in his car, while I was running
in a quiet neighborhood with old trees
            and cared-for yards.

Perhaps his wife had chased him out
she had thought she wanted another lover
and there was no room for him.
He packed a bag of clothes and thought he'd drive
somewhere, but spent the night sitting
behind the steering wheel
inside his car, parked in front of his house.

He didn't want to go anywhere
other than back inside

and he thought of getting the Sunday paper
but maybe he drifted into sleep
in the back of his mind he heard
what the radio was saying
he was thinking about getting laundry done
and about a restaurant where they had eaten
Chinese food last week

and he thought about his wife
and what lives they'd have if he never went back

later on, when the morning mist
rose up from the hills
hours after I had passed him sitting in his BMW
he went inside and looked at her

they both hadn't slept very much

the universe puts it this way

without question

THE PIANO AND SOMETHING ELSE

I sat down to play piano in San Jose
I thought the music would flow through me
my fingers towards the keys
            black and white
                something else
sinking down my shoulders
like words for poems
used in lobby phone calls
where a couple of women
are writing about their vacations
between gallery theater cafe

but the piano remained
under my fingers
heavy
treading
like climbing in the heart
without water slow sun
a full backpack
a piano and large mountain path
a grassy diamond
            the poem breathes into
                the words to another poem
a curve ball hovering right
in the strike zone
and I can hit it

this homerun symphony
Keith Jarrett, Mickey Mantle

heavy-pack hiker
heavy hitter
out for the long haul
this music that I sit down to play,

slashing shouts and vibrating voices
through fingers as keys listen
where I hustle
around the bases

I know that sound
the crack of the bat
and the field

HISTORY

The blue light sunset
and I pass by
everything in my car is dark
upon a road where Indians once gathered
across streams making acorn baskets,
acorn soup
where they lived before the train racketed
above an iron overpass,
where creeks met towards the Bay
and the night air flashes.

Cars converge at intersections
and the person in the car in front of me,
I imagine, he must be lost
his sense of direction swallowed by the silent dark,
familiar roads left behind.

My throat a musical humming along with the engine
softly, as I am drive near your house,

When I get in the door, the phone rings,
and I tell you, yes
I almost stopped by
that my life is a snapshot;
our friends and your children
photographs of uncertain smiles

We catch one another unaware
our way through dusk

blue night, any summer evening back home
A throat humming like frogs in the swampy night mist
that evening we circled the track, ten times
no resolution
just history

anytime I'd love your smile
just to continue

over the phone your voice is that risk
my car passing your house.

IN THE FIELD/ HAFSIKA

The field where we picked cotton in the Israeli Golan
Heights in the middle of the day with relentless sun
bearing over us, the bright glare piercing our eyes the
only shadows under the leaves of cotton plants and
our own figures walking and bending over through the
fields among the green rows picking weeds as heat
dripped off our bodies the sun at its zenith by noon,
we were given a break for fifteen minutes, "hafsika" in
the foreman's shack and a cup of thick Turkish coffee
and then back to the fields the long rows and rows of
green light shining off plants above the hard dry soil
with occasional puddle of irrigated water, mirage-like
in the profound heat and sunlight that had no
intention of letting up all day, just one big light
offered to us, as we would serve it and the crops,
bending to pull a weed and move on slowly,
deliberately to conserve necessary energy drained by
the heat in the intense kibbutz sun.

TEFILIN

A few months after Grandpa died, when I was thirteen, Grandma showed me his *tefilin*, the black leather box and straps and she told me he used it when he prayed. I had never seen him wearing the *tefilin*, although I had seen him at synagogue, in his talis and praying, davening, bending at the knees, beating his breast. She explained how he had to wrap it around his head and arm, but she didn't demonstrate this procedure and I imagined a kind of voluntary bondage that his religious devotion demanded. It was something he preferred in private or perhaps when he was at the orthodox congregation and I wouldn't have been able to see him there.

It then occurred to me to look up at the painting on the bedroom wall, a portrait of a rabbi, by Marc Chagall, if I remember correctly, which I had seen countless times, wearing *talis* and *tefilin* while holding his prayer books, looking out into the world of my grandparents. All these years I had wondered what exactly was on the man's arm and head, and here my grandfather actually had these special holy things too! He was like a rabbi! Grandma was busy shifting things around the room, getting boxes and *chotckes* out of the closet.

In that moment, when I was smelling and stroking the pieces of leather, I understood how each of us remains mysteriously and privately Jewish in our own temple of blessings and commitment.

DOMINICA

Animals by the roadside with chains
       around their necks,
not tied to anything
as I sleep through the morning rain
where gnarled roots cling to hillsides
and later, I bathe in the river while the sky still spits
a light drizzle, a blend of skin and earth's raw surface.

Children we pass want a ride in the car
and I point at the sunset when they ask for money:
"look, look, at the miracle that's free"
but they think I'm high on ganga
and maybe they can sell me more:
I watch the sun go down in their eyes.

Bob Marley gospel and Peter Tosh escapes
from the aluminum shanty shacks broken down
hardly restored after three years
when the hurricane winds ripped
the island's forests and houses out from the earth.

Muscled-backs, perfect postured
their bodies carry loads
while my legs absorb all the ruts in the road
One large bunch of bananas slung over my shoulder
pulls me out of shape.

In an open air lounge
with a whirling propeller fan
cricket moon over dark Caribbean Sea
contented spill of water, song of these hills.

I wait for the last shot of rum before bedtime.
Liquid swished around the glass as the ice cracks
open a body that holds the heart
of more than I know, jungle lush tropics
where rains have washed out the roads
and animals don't have to be tied down.

AMERICA AS A FOREIGN COUNTRY

"in this room you don't have to be perfect"
Sensai Kim, Aikido instructor

In this room we learn the center
of conversation like a martial art
and we are clumsy
with the movement

in this room
we drift in and out like air
sometimes the lights are on
sometimes they're off

sometimes the window is open

in this room
the breath wanders like a mistake in grammar
in this room, I keep thinking that talking loud or slow
makes them understand
"up for grabs", "drop in" "bump into"
all the expressions I gesture

the students come and go reading
newspapers and advertisements
and they have their opinions about America
and learning English
and what I give them to go on

they go on
as tourists or return to their home country

where their future has been mapped out and directed

just a side trip, this summer
a holiday in America and a chance to learn English

the students like to sleep late
they have student visas
they don't have to come to class
but they will get reprimanded of course if they don't

often they come to class hungover or high

I consult my dictionary

"accolades", "cooperation", "corporation"
"democracy", "melee", "trashed"

"dynamic", from "dunamikos", "power"

"interesting, nice, boring, beautiful"
these words, which I explain, don't describe—
the qualities of that life outside this room

In this room you just have to get by

All the idioms balled up into a baseball game
a ball of wax
the whole shebang
a thread of knots
the six-pack in the closet

the students go on trips to Yosemite or Santa Cruz
they go shopping in San Francisco
they can go off by themselves if they wish
but many are afraid of getting lost
and having to find their way
back to the room
where they don't have to know the answers
where the teacher doesn't know the answers

 I consult the grammar book

or I look out the window,
the globe spinning beneath us;
and it's summertime

or I just look at them.

while down the street, homeless, headlines
and violence a filth that's indifferent,
just like their country

a world full of imperfection and contradictions.

that make us beautiful

Part Three

MASS TRANSIT

Some kids say this man just died
        while sitting on the bus
slumped over while they played music
and cracked jokes, and everyone is talking about
the man who was stabbed
on the train yesterday when he interfered,
some loudmouth punks hassling other passengers.

Kids from Catholic school wearing plaid,
skirts and ties
Kids going home from San Francisco
wearing leather and chains
black t-shirts and boots, lacquered hair,
earrings through their noses.
Commuters clutching their brief cases
and Diet Coke cans, tattered ingredients,
battered packages,
pressed shirts and skirts stumble in and out
which way to exit the clouds

Back and forth on the train, underground
and elevated rails pass over yards of truckstops and
sweatshops, clotheslines
junk heaps, snarling parking lot dogs
under clear skies of all that belligerence
the smell of human sweat, excrement in corners

Last night in the train there was a fight
drug dealers and players,
masses of chairs and choirs ritual street alley prayers

where the bridge or freeway could come down.

Someone has left their dead banana to rot
among the heaps of newspapers
where a dirty young man sleeps, sprawled out
in workclothes, dirty red sweat pants,
greasy hightops over the seat in front of him.

A tourist family boards, the teenage girl looks
nothing like her parents; she watches the guy
stretched out - other passengers look up
at the father's fat angry voice,
the embarrassed girl and annoyed mother, mumble
to one another, and the father yells out
"Mind your own business"
then the mother and daughter move down the train
to switch seats

and the young man shifts in his sleep.

JOURNEYS ARE A WAY OF MARKING OUT A DISTANCE...

Weldon Kees

Where is Weldon Kees? They say he disappeared
in San Francisco,
but maybe he's still traveling the country
back and forth, like a ping pong ball
stopping at filling stations and roadside business,
working when he can, tending rowboats
        at summer camps.
What proof is there of his disappearance?
Perhaps he's fishing in a foggy inlet or
finishing chores quietly in the mountains.
maybe he has a shack nestled within a rugged
seaside cove where he writes his memoirs.
He could be working in a second class hotel
keeping track of the towels,
the sun pounding on the deck;
maybe he folds the linens and fills tin foil
        with pastries.
Maybe he's sitting in a cabin like this one in Bolinas
watching cattail grasses shake diligently
as overgrown bushes of berries mangle themselves into
gnarled trees embraced by vines.
He may be writing poetry, sending it to *APR* and
collecting rejection slips.
At the Bandon lighthouse he surveys the sea
and the isolation of sculptured coast,
rock worn down by the water.
Maybe he has chosen anonymity and a business in
New York City

but now, as a retired executive with a retreat upstate—
he's just seventy years old and entertains society,
they take him by the elbow
and help him up the stairs.
Or maybe because he's in love with America,
he doesn't last long in one place
he turns over pages in his calendar
and looks for springtime,
watches the Vermont mountains dotted with skiers
while he sips sherry and reads for the fifth time
          his copy of *The White Goddess*.
Maybe there's a young woman who helps him
          while he cooks a catch
of fresh fish from Long Island,
or he's sucking a piece of straw along the freeway
as he's hitchhiking through the cornfields
or he's driving a cab
and no one knows how old he is
sitting next to you
in a cafe,
in San Francisco.

NANCY'S AUCTION FOR HER SON SAM'S RAINFOREST

In the early evening breeze,
insect buzz
like a bunch of friends that never ends

and he was such a great swimmer
how could he drown?

A hollow sound from whirlpool shadows
a crumpled breath

light in the rain
something on her mind
something time won't heal

the answer always right behind her back
the jungle encloses
like friends crowding a school lunchroom
a direction within her glance,
eyes that go on and on like a poem.

A whale on shore
a dead boy in the rain forest
a room full of quiet toys
a poster of Marilyn Monroe
she wants to get rid of her jackets
and clothes and books
and furniture
everything that seems too expensive or useless
hand-me-downs

another style she doesn't fit anymore.

a spike in the back
a shelf of unread books
a knife in the heart
        tools for Christ
        close up shop

handfuls of water
a forest thicketed with ancestors

his body a net of secrets
stories, brilliance, convulsion
a cheerleader
a tender echo

as the trees weep   the rain keeps going.

At sunset, birdcalls
parakeets through the windows
difficult moon on the walk down
neighborhood familiar streets
cross at the stop sign, stay in the yellow lines

the force of his body
twisting seeds into trees
salamanders wander up roots and wings

take him home.

MENNA'S DREAM

You are homeless wandering Times Square with an
unrecognizable child in your arms, her body and yours
shivering together in the night until they find you and
take you to what turns out to be your home, where
you have lived and raised your child, you just needed
help there was some confusion about what was yours
and the need you had to be cared for by others, you
were lost in your hometown, not really yours to
possess but neighborhoods have that family instinct,
and you had been searching for something to keep you
and the child together, as the dream reveals what
you'd regret if you hadn't birthed this child.

How lost we are, people on the street find some way
to feed themselves, yet no one can do it alone, what
the city has forgiven surfaces an intimacy with
strangers through a collage of selves pasted together in
sleep, the secrets emerge that need to take care of,
that urge to be cared for even though the child in your
arms doesn't look like you she's silent and courageous
as she glares into city lights and her eyes reach
towards those who might scare you and they find you
and shelter you they take you back.

BUSINESS OF POETRY

at the violet hour, when the eyes and back
turn upward from the desk, when the human engine
waits
Like a taxi throbbing waiting
                    T.S. Eliot   The Wasteland

when it's quitting time
when the restless ache of your day is behind
a ray of sun
when the computer screen bubbles into an aquarium
when the lights have been dimmed
into the dusk of post ventilation air
when it's happy hour
when it's time to close the ledger
close the tally sheet and phone log
when it's time to pack up
and lock up shop
when you stretch for your gym bag
and pour yourself into sweat shorts and tee-shirt
a tied bundle of newspapers
an emptied trash of wadded nerves
when it's time to go
time to make the train
make it to the bank before closing
and finally make it home
when it's only a job when it's only the poem
with its accounts of what
you later will open up to.

(she was) ABLE TO SAY

for each she was able to say and be sure that meeting
something being herself, the language of dogs of the
people waiting outside the community church. that
they are waiting for soup she could say or learn how
to speak the language of dogs so that the dogs would
follow her home or she could make decisions and
decide something anything where to go for lunch or
dinner or which show to attend with her friend for
herself she was able to say and be sure she wanted
these days to be new and different even though
without wanting each day could be new and finally
lonely or able to say lovely darling and to love the
something that she was waiting for hardly a day passed
when she couldn't wait to decide or learn or make a
language and decide on soup for lunch. that she
wanted soup or she wanted to wait for something to
make a decision not to be lonely or hungry but to be
loved and to speak a language that someone could
understand if she could decide to speak it she would
have to decide and have to wait at the same time
being the same being for each one of these things
she was able to say and be sure about meeting the
new thing being made inside herself that she was
waiting for that wanted to be said

after Gertrude Stein and Leslie Scalapino

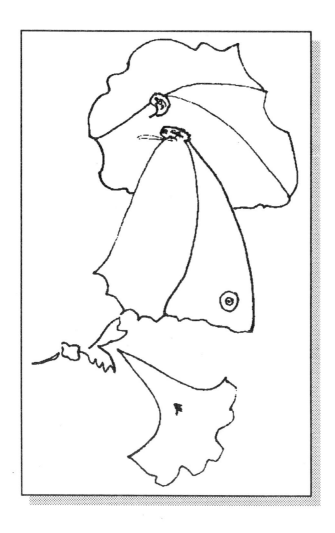

Part Four

The ritual of Fridays, tourists and workers
hurried to meet for drinks
take the worry out
a place where the shape of feelings
is song, lifting glasses the edge of light
packing clothes and landscapes into bundles
the words by heart
something left unsaid
out of a novel, I desire home-cooking
and sentimental arrangements
but forced by anonymity
into the risks of language I make.

WAITING AGAIN

what else is there but patient light
drifting I recklessly roam the streets
where no one else has ever been
through a certain breeze and forgetfulness
wondering how else to go
watching the traffic and silence of feet
men on the lookout for one another
anxiously, I look up
my eyes wet
the light they become

Their problems and struggles are ordinary, even if they
are rich. Two white Samoyeds sitting in the car, a late
model luxury sedan, chocolate brown, creamy leather
interior. The car parked in front of the nightclub and
the owner is thinking about them, that they are hot,
hungry and tired from being dragged around all day.
We have qualities that they admire too, as well as
what they deplore. Our mediocrity for any car that
runs, mixed breeds. We choose the lives of the rich in
hopes of mirage, they give is what they think we want,
flashy parties, gossip columns, expensive habits,
lifestyle of the rich and famous, national inquirer, Liz
Smith, the morning paper what people blab about.

We enjoy flirting and storytelling. The illusion of being
dipped into the motivations of other lives, our
fantasies replaced by well-delineated pain. We'd rather
be voyeurs than act out our own agony, desires, the
attention we give, looking out the closest windows.

The Zen Buddhists believe that they problem is
separation, as the water falls from the mountain to
join the river, it is separated from all the other drops,
that slow falling

into the current, whatever has happened to make a
person an artist, a drop of water on its own, fragile
and discontinuous, tugged by the demands of
character, development, association and stumbling into
the discovery we like the falling

When the singer emerges from the darkness we feel relaxed. There's a shared misery in her eyes, but she's reflecting on some experience we know is private we know it in her voice, a river of smoky light and piano jazz, that ordinary urge to fold the napkin in our laps, to suck on the sizzle stick and remember to let the dogs out of the car.

she is looking down
at her feet
in the rain
she's completely drenched
she can't decide whether or not to cross the street
the pavement rises up to her
and way past the clouds

where the space shuttle Columbia
reaches out
for satellite experiment rendezvous
five years late outer space

the silly lady can hardly find some dry place
out of the rain
the dogs bark at her over the fence
panhandlers keep asking her for change,
car horns blast as she steps off the curb and back
until finally someone steers her inside
after a few wet hours on the street

and sets down a steaming mug of coffee
as she mumbles thankfully,
watching
someone reading today's paper
front page space mission
information about the universe
and exploring

She looked so good in her red dress and make-up

I had been riding my bike before sunset and stopped
by the bookstore reception;
in the dusky rose sunset of neighborhoods,
up a on little rise, clear enough to see the City.

Later, draining a beer glass, dust on my books,
cobwebs between bicycle spokes, intricate silky
patterns linking the juniper tree
          and battered redwood fence slats,
I entered the house in time to help with dinner.

Contemplating a train journey,
          dining cars then nomads in wagons
challenged by moving or staying in one place,
pastures of cows and field,
a long way to keep going

In the yard, weeds shoot around my legs,
early starlight glimmer through erratic fog
following indifferent voices and a deep patience.

What will you write
I wonder while you've spent days
planting in your sunny front yard
or biking with kids by the Bay;
when you've finished shopping
then cooking and dinner dishes
after tucking the kids in
finally relaxing on the couch, your arm stretched out
to the man you've married while he watches TV.

There's the chance you'll write about the deep sky
one star, one moon
clearly within reach—
when I had linked my arm into yours,
and you touched my hand.

Is this the poem you'll write or is it mine?
Clothing and schoolbooks scattered in the hallway
notes and checks and newspapers
        among breakfast dishes;

there's space between a framed picture and the wall.

Just seasons enough and not yet spring—
a whisper of fog musing over the trees
around the clutter of our lunch picnic
and hoping to get warm, today I pressed
my hands against your knees,
a prayer.

DELIVERANCE

I arrive with your mail almost midnight
and sit your porch
overhead the range of starlight
homes twinkling in the distance
shuddering in my own body
      and no lights in your house
I wrestle with everything I am
not to disturb you; although I want to terribly,
I don't.

As I scrunch up my face into a voice
that yowls profound sadness, an anguish
that I do everything to avoid since you left me,
there used to be things I could hold that held me
but now I'm not sure.

I start writing on the envelop how much I miss you
and that I'm so sorry...
but I'm not sorry. I cross that out.
I just leave it "I miss you"
even though I know it's not really you I miss
because for so long we missed each other
we stopped being close
we stopped the caring
we had become too comfortable,
and I guess I miss having someone who knows me.

As I throw the bundle of letters onto your porch
the echo slaps against the old wood
into the empty street,

I get up from the stairs and decide
to drive to the pool hall and make a few shots
that give me confidence.

and then I drive home
too much to drink, and amazed that I made it.

I'm heading home toward the unknown:
the pool cue is memory, a practice of my body
and intellect and luck, I guess
an angle of myself reaching
some shots are like the stars
surprising and glowing
some of them I can see how it's possible,
but I still miss them.
and some I never figure out
I can't tell what could've been different
to make it in the sky
stars constellated and the balls randomly flung
against the bumpers and each other
and this person on your porch just happened
there, last Sunday in the quiet city night
then after a few shots of pool
drifted home

BREAKING APART

cool breath of light before sunset
fragments shine through the trees
that explode with fluttering in the winged air
the sound of birds in the distance
and cars echo on the road
voices of people you might know or never see again
the rumbling over a hill or in the sky a little airplane
churning and cows making their way through
the slump of mud and your vague desires.

a frog starts croaking in the swamp;
overhead chattering birds an awareness of what flesh
requires breaking sound and light;
reading the road you choose when running
or sleeping out in the wet grass
clad only in a tee-shirt and underwear
the dogs may awaken you
but you'd be happy to be lost
in that mist rising over the grass
or light sprinkling from hillside glare
in the twittering that illuminates the last
folly into darkness, that will to marvel at the breaking
of stone bending of grass underfoot— pebbles rolling—
and knowing that only the moment glistens
in your isolation and sureness

how the magnificence of the view could anywhere
lasting like brave flight
the sliver of moon poking
through pale sky as the day ends,

taken for granted taken for itself
logs and mulch and vibrating shadows on the field;

the woods darken, the world muddies, breaks apart
while you never see or hear it the drip of dead leaves
and fading sharp soft light

as the moon's white crescent cuts
and glows into the sky
and one car pummels the road
a bird advances through a spindly tree
the frog grows into a night voice gray trees moist
stillness.

woodpecker tapping another bird call
the long light leaving shadows
vibrating softness around the privilege of creatures
            and countryside
changing just by chance and breaking

open your heart

DESCARTES

Starting from scratch, the slate wiped clean,
just the desire
your plan for future, or maybe you don't want one
the fresh ocean in the morning, children making kites
the beach just starting to hum with bargains
a hunger you want to savor, a knot in the line
the curve of her body in the room
        that has known many feelings such as these;
the jungle over the hill
the cobblestone streets,
the families who make ends meet
and the clatter of everyone speaking a language
they'll never understand
the secret of desire that makes your mind fresh
and curious

Tobey Kaplan

Tobey Kaplan, a poet originally from New York City, has been teaching in the San Francisco Bay Area for over seventeen years. She is an active member of California Poets in the Schools, and regularly conducts creative writing and poetry workshops in public schools and publishes anthologies of student writing at the end of each school year.

Ms. Kaplan received grants from the California Arts Council, 1979-1982 to serve as poet in residence at community mental health centers, and has also taught creative writing as an adult education instructor at county jail facilities. She has also worked as detention facilities tutor coordinator for a library-based literacy program. She is an artist in residence advocate and works as a consultant, assisting arts and education programs in developing artist-based workshops and artist-teacher partnerships. Tobey Kaplan currently teaches Basic Composition at Ohlone Community College in Fremont, and Business Literature and Professional Writing at the University of Phoenix-Northern California Campus. Ms. Kaplan has given workshops and presentations throughout the country regarding creative process, literacy and progressive social/cultural empowerment through poetry.

Ms. Kaplan received an B.A. degree, English/Creative Writing Concentration from Syracuse University, 1975 and her M.A. in Interdisciplinary Studies, Creative Arts from San Francisco State University, 1983.

She performed her work in variety of venues, including Intersection for the Arts in San Francisco, St. Mark's Poetry Project in New York City, City Books in Pittsburgh, PA and Powell's Books in Portland, OR. She has been published in numerous literary magazines and anthologies. A limited edition chapbook *No Turning Back* appeared from e.g. press in 1984.

In January 1986, she was selected as a resident fellow for Dorland Mountain Colony and has served on the Program Committee for Small Press Distribution in Berkeley. Ms. Kaplan has also been a screener for the SF Bay Guardian Poetry Contest, and was a third place prize-winner in the 1993 Chester H. Jones Foundation National Poetry Competition for her poem, Descartes. Recently, she has been chosen to join the Headlands Center For The Arts as an affiliate resident, and nominated for an Oakland Business Arts award as an Arts Education Advocate 1995.